RECIPROCAL DISTILLATIONS

RECIPROCAL DISTILLATIONS

CLAYTON ESHLEMAN

HOT WHISKEY PRESS

RECIPROCAL DISTILLATIONS

Cover Painting: Ischian Sphinx by Leon Golub.
Used with permission by Spero Golub Family LLC.

ISBN 0-9786933-0-2
Library of Congress Control Number: 2006934575

Hot Whiskey Books are available through Small Press Distribution
or directly from the publisher.

www.hotwhiskeypress.com
Hot Whiskey Press ❖ Boulder, CO

In Memory of Bill Paden

ACKNOWLEDGEMENTS

Some of these poems (and the note on "Spirits of the Head") appeared, occasionally in different versions, in the following magazines: *American Poetry Review*, *Brooklyn Rail*, *Poésie* (Paris), *Action Restreinte* (Paris), *New American Writing*, *Possum Pouch* website, *Mandorla*, *Arson*, *Fascicle*, *Vanitas*, and *Ygdrasil* website.

"Figure and Ground," "Corot, 1870," "Michaux, 1956," "Spirits of the Head," and "Darger" were published in *Everwhat* (Zasterle Books, La Laguna-Tenerife, Canary Islands, 2003).

"A Shade of Paden" was produced as a booklet by David Sellers for Pied Oxen Printers, Hopewell, New Jersey, 2006.

"Darger," "Corot, 1870," and "The Beheading" were researched in Chicago, Reims (France) and Valletta (Malta) with Graduate School Research Support from Eastern Michigan University. My gratitude to Robert Holkeboer, Dean of the Graduate School, who made this support possible.

"Clayton Eshleman: Taking It Out, Painting It In" was originally published by the online literary journal, *Fascicle*.

CONTENTS

CLAYTON ESHLEMAN: TAKING IT OUT, PAINTING IT IN
by Roberto Tejada

Image density is the salient feature that renders poetic space distinct in Clayton Eshleman's animation of a language that allows for thick terms of concentration and complex shadings. This is to speak of degrees that extend back and forth, from comic-strip plain form, in emphatic warps of surface effect, to the half-light and roundedness of things no more than partially disclosed as heretofore sealed inside a cave; and this should come as no surprise from a writer who for over forty years in a commitment to poetry and intellectual life has thought intensely about history and its various objects, counting those we differentiate as art. These *Reciprocal Distillations* are a reminder, too, of how much critical potential there is in acts of admiration and the ability to honor the artistry of other makers, forebears and fellow travelers alike.

Eshleman achieves the foregoing in diverse rehearsals of a poetic subgenre that bears his unmistakable signature, in writing that performs the mediations of both maker and viewer: the dialogic lyric of the beholder. The poems here re-stage the personal and social struggles materialized in objects whose present time is manifestly out of place with the historic moment of a prior making, and because discontinuous—in an imperative sense thereby largely unassailable—Eshleman's writing about them explodes into moments of proliferating aesthetic reflection, and into mineral layerings that are the wagers of language in relation to History: "What is broken advances, / pillowed by what will not yield: / a thought drinking its shadow" ("Joan Mitchell's Spinnerets," p. 41).

Forebears and fellow travelers alike: Clayton's history of the image has unearthed an enabling narrative in the Upper Paleolithic, insofar as the poet gives name to such a "construction of the underworld." But this telling is not an origin story, nor a starting point identical to itself; it is a strangely familiar place that accounts for the social and political night terrors that are the human species becoming other to animal organization by means of mimesis and image-making. In "Chauvet, Left Wall of End Chamber" Eshleman submits what follows as a note-to-self and challenge to the archeologist: "Check this: / animal holocaust in the late Ice Age / corresponds with the rise of war." The suggestive nature of Clayton's assertion does not end there; he interrogates the metaphors of art historical conviction with regard to the Upper Paleolithic, not as evidence or trace of *Homo sapiens* being separate or distinct from our anterior selves. Instead, Eshleman telescopes prehistory into the present so as to make visible the structure of political life in the modern age by dint of our representations. ["Rhino with 8 oversized curving parallel horns / as if drawn by Marcel Duchamp. / *Rhino Descending a Lion Stare*" (p. 29).] The art historian and theorist Donald Preziosi suggests a link between what is at stake in the conventional art historical account of prehistory with the modern theory of mind when he writes: "In some way, our picture of earlier humans has always been conflated with our observations of our own children—the notion that human ontogeny, or infant development, recapitulates or repeats stages of human phylogeny or evolution" [Preziosi 1989, 143.] Eshleman tells that his attention to the visual derived from reading "funnies" in the Indiana newspapers of his childhood, from comic books and his own early efforts at cartoon-strip depiction.

The particularly modernist account that is psychoanalysis provides a foundational model for describing the development of the self and such objects of human exchange and expenditure as to give continued shape to individuation. As a system, it looks to practices that deviate from the sexual or social norm, to the baffling exceptions that are literature and art, to states of behavior altered by the social order or otherwise induced— by neurosis, through perversion, or under pharmaceutical influence. An evolutionary method for understanding cultural production, it can look to a maker's biography, to her historic moment, and to something defined loosely as the temperament colliding between the two. As Sara

Kofman reminds us, Freud suggested also a structural method for relating forces and phenomena to each other in such resonance as may be found in the otherwise unexamined detail. This circular interpretation makes it possible for a non-unified or absent historic identity to be structured as a breathing subject. It relies on certain assumptions: that truth is revealed in its distortions; that it is constructed from displacements or substitutions; and that there is no first-order artwork referring only to itself, but rather to the never-ending play of second-order effects. It's a technique Eshleman deploys in some of his most insightful readings of art in poetic form. He looks at the Biblical tableaux of Caravaggio, the monumental figures of Leon Golub, the psychic girl-legion battlefields of outsider artist Henry Darger, and the exhaustive drawings of visionary Unica Zürn. This last artist, still largely under-appreciated, was the companion of Hans Bellmer in Paris from 1953 to 1970, the year of Zürn's death by defenestration, and Eshleman affords her sometimes drug-induced work a primary place of its own.

Eshleman's poems in general, but those on artworks in particular, begin with a premise that for the knowable to be known it must undergo a necessary and always reiterated "de-arranging" at the moment we render it representable. At a recent live reading, Eshleman's framing device to the poem devoted here to Unica Zürn serves as paradigm for his own writerly practice—and as the primary contest for commentators of his own poetic singularity—when he claims that "[Zürn's] work is incredibly, richly interior, with lots of moves that are not describable; so it's an interesting challenge to try to articulate stuff like this that you're really [...] having to invent phrasings and words for" [Kelly Writer's House, University of Pennsylvania: October 19, 2005.][1] The predominance of eye imagery that composes the tissues of Zürn's scrawled fields give way to a series of improvisations lending particular valence, for example, to the first line of the passage below—the word "tear" doubling over into lachrymal conduit precisely as it opens up into cleft or slash.

[1]This reading is available at the following link: http://writing.upenn.edu/pennsound/x/Eshleman.html

To travel within Unica's tear, to view the celestial
viper-vibrational
xylophone of her mind, the cartwheel
cocoliths of her insectile-thronging dark.
Eyes as trowels.
Raccoon nautiloids in millipedal waver.

("Unica Zürn," p. 56)

Eshleman's interrogations of the formal qualities that animate Zürn's brand of image-making are an invitation for the poet himself to turn comparable inflections of excess, dizzying gradations of sense and sound that produce both a readerly turbulence—"xylophone of her mind, the cartwheel / cocoliths of her insectile-thronging dark"—and the lightheaded exhilaration of overload. In those moments of pleasure and stress, Eshleman's aesthetic—together with the choice and range of artists he engages—defies our conventional notions of decorum. The vocal axis of the poem unhinges, too, off the organizing cadence of the poet-speaker to assume the subject position of the artworks' producer—the "viper-vibrational" self of a projected "Zürn" thrashing back into the poem's transitory middle-voice again. [In live performances, Clayton inhabits to great effect a de-centered speech: a sort of cartoon gigantism attached to certain phrasings in order to perform the split that exists between the rationally argued and that which decomposes at the point of saturation.]

To turn to this poem a propos of Zürn is to acknowledge the peculiar brand of surrealism to which Eshleman is heir—a lineage that points simultaneously back to Europe (Artaud, Bataille), Latin America, and the Caribbean (Vallejo, Césaire). We can look to the very suggestive writings of Roger Caillois—a figure whose intellectual commitments as well joined Europe and Latin America—to illuminate the relationship between "personality" and "space," so crucial to Eshleman's poetics. Caillois claims that insofar as I can assimilate into my surroundings, there is a decline in my feelings of personal attributes. To the degree that I generalize space, the more distinct become my feelings of mental and somatic sovereignty. So, the fate of indulging with fantasy may lead to such mimetic incorporation of the animate in the inanimate, and vice versa, as to engender progenies disfigured by the imagination. Enabled by Caillois, art historian Rosalind Krauss has thus argued that surrealist doubling is, fittingly, an invasion of the body by space. In light of the art objects that compel his attention, Eshleman's practice constitutes a kind of invasion of the poet's imagined body—the "phantom anatomy" of psychoanalysis—by the idealized quantity projected into the historic nexus of interpretation between the beholder and beheld for which the poem is an analog. Consider the following lines occasioned by figures in the Dapper Museum of African Art, Paris:

> If, over my tall blue pearled neck, I stare in terror, it is because
> foxes have gotten inside me,
> foxes are tearing apart my death.
>
> Pitch-black head breaking out in red currants, in spikes, in blisters,
> head a field sprouting buds, pebbles, studs,
> head issuing a living waving horn,
> head asleep, head replete, head whose dream matrix pustulates
> the prayer of all things: to emerge, at once.
>
> ("Witchery," p. 1)

The space of writing together with the nascent shapes of the mediating objects forge the site of a dialogue: in a language by which the act of viewing itself is incited, interrogated, seductively teased, and argued with. Eshleman likewise discovers in each poem the form and word-tone commensurate with his subject. Reflexive phonic textures match the quietude of the painter's vision in "Corot, 1870" (p. 14). Elsewhere, verbal designs are drafted in relation to the calligraphic paintings of contemporary Syrian artist Khaled Al-Saa'i so as to mimic a modulation that

> ...sees nature as intelligible word lore mortal scored rims
> or rhymes, a lingo ribbonesque with inner din
> (questers sounding themselves
> off stone in a darkness sparkling with
> ghoul-infested whirligigs...

("Radix," p. 39)

This poem ends with a description not only of its subject but of its own emergence— as well "a lacework of letter flavor cometary clover!" Close examination of that particular last line, its prosodic stress (• | • • | • • • | • • • | •) and the range of what its references suggest, yields the "interlocking sway" of the "alpha radiant omega" linking galaxy to blade of grass, genesis to spiral terminus, and choice to complexity. With a resemblance now and then to Elias Canetti's *Agony of Flies*, Eshleman's poetry lends aphoristic care to the philosophical promise of fauna in chromatic scale: that is, of animals and colors as primary terms that can be interchangeable: "Once razed, the mind's hive releases mastodontal honey" ("Michaux, 1956," p. 16).

In the end, however, it is this poetry's relevance to art history I want to argue. As Mikhail Bakhtin claimed of the novel, poetry too has the ability to enfold and incorporate other genres and media, but this has been much less the case for what classifies as art-historical discourse. The degrees to which art histories claim a scientific detachment may serve as the alibi for disciplinary investments in "naturalizing and validating the very *idea* of art as 'universal' human phenomenon [... art history being] a powerful *instrument* for imagining and scripting the social, cognitive and ethical histories of all peoples" [Preziosi 1998, 18.] Without forfeit of so-called art-historical "accuracy," the limberness of poetic discourse considering the strict partitions of subject and object, of self and other, provides empirical agency for a palpable, wider-reaching knowledge; and the kind of intuitive leaps that only a poem can make available are in such excess of standard academic remarks as to offer sufficient counter-statement to so much lackluster scholarship. These moments of poetic elucidation cannot be generalized, nor are they easily earned, nor are they often possible to isolate without injury to the overarching argument or to such abundant phenomena specific to the lyric genre.

Joan Mitchell once claimed, "The word blank is what bothers me. It has no image to it. B L A N K. It's nothing, something on a typewriter; or a mind that's nowhere [...] To me figure/ground means the use of space. [...] Now if I have a blank space in there and it isn't working as a positive space, as well as an unpainted space then I'll take it out or paint it in" [Cohen, p. 22.] It is art-historically coherent for Eshleman to inaugurate his poem "Joan Mitchell's Spinnerets" with a description of the painter's brushstrokes as "[w]hite flowers scissor-billowing the hemlock;" it is consistent not only within the logic of that metaphor but operates as a figure of speech proper to the cut and swell, the action of carving by way of enlargement, that constitutes a brush technique resistant to the negative dialectic of the blank painterly field. To a historic Mitchell's "blank is what bothers me," the poet's surrogate Mitchell proffers a "blob of vermillion and a swath of no." This attention to a subtractive mathematics coloring an otherwise value-added brushstroke—negative, positive: "take it out, paint it in"—is especially relevant given the sexual politics of post-war art production in the United States, largely masculine in its social formation and patriarchal in its tenor. Here and elsewhere, Eshleman shows scholarly interest in questions posed similarly by T. J. Clark with a view to the logic of abstract expressionism. What makes one brushstroke successful, and another not? Of Mitchell's overarching critical implications the poet asks:

> Whose death mask is being molded with
> these rampant arctotheric clouds?

How divine the state of the union in
the entrails of
Daisy Mae?

("Joan Mitchell's Spinnerets," p. 44)

This conclusion, its coloring applied in layered dashes, requires a brief annotation of terms: "arctotheric" being a reference to the short-faced bear common to North America; Daisy Mae Scragg, the voluptuously rendered heroine of *Li'l Abner*, Al Capp's popular U.S. comic strip of the early to mid-twentieth century. The artwork is that holdout surviving the contact zone, Eshleman claims, of the material world in the face of demise; that this confluence should take place in the bowels of a mass-culture representation is nothing short of inspired; it's also release from a tragic masquerade, for in the comic strip Daisy Mae represents a prison house of femininity so long as her agency remains largely unrecognized and unrewarded. To view Mitchell's kind of nonfigurative practice at the slippage of what compels the lexis of *death mask, cloud, state of the union,* and *entrails,* is to analogize even as it is to insinuate the nuclear menace that determined what an entire generation of so-called New York School artists could make legible in paint. To this, Eshleman blows wide open the forceful work of Leon Golub with the political inquiry: "If abstract color fields are peeled away, / What terrors will show through?" This question is posed as an "or else" in the same poem regarding Golub's series of full-canvas fighting male nudes:

How much degradation can an image take
and still, scraped into and from the canvas itself, manifest
this world's lethal embrace? The age
demanded an image, right? ok? here it is:
man as ruined monumentality.

("Monumental," p. 59)

The terrors for which the distortions of caricature serve as social compensation lead the poet to probe the visionary work of Henry Darger in an attempt to address the problem of pathology in art and mental life: "Why was Darger Darger?" Indeed, Eshleman sees the psychoanalytic struggle of a subject in excess of itself not as a fin-de-siécle parlor drama but once again as a peculiarly U.S. American cartoon or gazette motif. The cartoon's visual economy of perverse form and overstatement is the visual equivalent for a social temperature that necessitates asking, "Is paradise the absence of adults?" In the poem, a catalog of the titles comprising Darger's personal library remains unembellished, but its "order of disclosure"—George Oppen's celebrated words—provides an indelible version of the man who owned them and leads to the following first-person identification, a kind of knowledge that a scholarly account could not possibly contain:

> I am Chicago Weather, Hendro Darger the Volcanologist,
> author of a 15,000 page novel, Pepto-Bismol bottle collector,
> I rescue crucifixes from trash cans,
> my eyeglasses held together by tape,
> wallet tied to shoestring attached to belt loop.
> Jesus, are you a little girl? Jesus, am I in
> your body? Nail-wracked Jesus,
>   am I your daughter
>   self?
>
> ("Darger," p. 22)

I cannot resist quoting the final couplet of this poem, not only because it is emblematic of Eshleman's style, but because its joyousness derives too from the fact that such effects are impossible in any other medium beyond that of embodied speech or the "vocal utopias" so dear to Michel de Certeau, not always pacific and describable perhaps likewise as a

Comic strip valley aswarm with cradle-shaped rangers.
Radiant sweetness shotgun emptied into dot-eyed zombies.

("Darger," p. 19)

About the life and work of Caravaggio, "The Beheading" is an art story in the stressed fabric of language, tightly woven and teeming with psychologically consistent kinks and snags. Crisscrossing between the biographical account, visual analysis, and psychoanalytic examination—and delving into the great homosexual themes to which the Biblical figures of David, Goliath, John the Baptist and Christ can correspond—the poem tenders a startling syllogism: the potential for buggery is to the fear of castration what the real political threat of decapitation was to the various Caravaggio renderings of "Salomé with the Baptist's Head" and "David with the Head of Goliath." Eshleman links the artist's obsession with beheadings to a formal strategy in as much as Caravaggio's survival was contingent upon repressing erections in his painting. It's a poem that shows Eshleman's range as a writer not only of wild lyric lines of flight but of relaxed phrasings confident also in argument and exposition.

I want to return now to the place where I began: to Clayton's demanding image-structure and thus to a poem that summarizes his particular poetics as a theory of art. To account for the rendering of the deity Ganesha, the short poem "Obstacle Breaker" alters the initial terms to make the figure's elephant trunk a living organism reproduced asexually, a birth requiring only one parent, generative method of the gods:

Parthenogenetic

uroboros. Take a self-subtracted
art from me. Feed your adder.

You are mist.

("Obstacle Breaker," p. 27)

The adder, or northern viper, coils here at a two-fold remove: one that permits the technologies of a self to withhold or abstract the substance that it simultaneously adjoins and suspends in the act of image making. For wordsmith and image-maker alike, what artworks and poetry in dialogue allow is that to devour one art form or series is, paradoxically, to begin to give birth to the other. One of our founding art historians, Aby Warburg, for whom the serpent was an image of agency and causality, at least in his marvelously idiosyncratic reading of the Pueblo Indian practices, wrote in 1923 that: "Human culture evolves toward reason in the same measure as the tangible fullness of life fades into a mathematical symbol" [Iversen, 221.] For Eshleman the sign of a self-devouring and self-generating serpent, representative of the negative/positive space of exchange between what we see and what we say, loom as though attainable for an instant even as it fades likewise into mist. Warburg's writing is exemplary for art history: it recognized that there can exist an "object" of art only insofar as it is contingent and intertwined; self-proclaimed disinvestment in any description will be reliant always on a first-person immediacy, inevitably suppressed, but in whose encounter subject and object are for a moment indistinguishable.

Caught in the stress point between a kind of materialism and ideal constituted in the double acts of expenditure and conception, Eshleman reveals the appetite of a realist. Writes the critic Keith Tuma: "It is as if the poetry must be as complex and crowded—as agonized, hilarious, confused, lucid, derivative, singular, as full of farts, food, and ecstasies—as life itself" [Tuma, 180.] But fueling this corporeal reality principle is a kind of utopianism that sees community in art as an ethical archetype. Throughout *Reciprocal Distillations* there is a touching sense, one of wonder before the state of our present history, that art is even possible at all or that its makers have, in actuality, lived among us. To the fact that they are often friends Eshleman pays tribute in poems on work of contemporaries as far and wide as Bill Paden, Nora Jaffe, Leon Golub, Nancy Spero, and Ana

Mendieta. Increasingly more symptomatic of our cultural climate is the reality that present-day agents of visual practice in the United States are aware almost not at all that poetry can be an equally critical rehearsal to assess the value of visual meaning. That poets likewise speak with scarce authority to the contemporary art world and its complex association with the market economy is hardly encouraging given a suggestion that "visual studies is helping, in its own modest, academic way, to produce subjects for the next stage of globalized capital" [Alpers, 25.] Evidence points to a transnational capital that is inclined rather to make us more and more specialized so as to further solidify barriers in communication across technical and disciplinary boundaries.

Eshleman beckons the drive that uniformly animates the objects of art as well as the subjects of its history—at that "interlocking sway" of manufacture and reception, between a spectator's encounter and the broader social project of evaluating value. He deploys the visual object and the varieties of its potential meanings to galvanize the very specific effects of the poetic medium as such in poems whose model is that of the dialogue—as much a song for two voices resembling the address of erotic love and discord, as it is an appeal for instruction: How next to speak? In an unremitting imperative that so turns the visual inside out as to make it a series of written figures possible only at the level of the spoken is built the ethics of an appetite whose multi-part arrangement refutes conventional distinctions of form and content, of the public and private. These lyric works endure at last to claim a case in point that poets might have something relevant to contribute to the cultural conversation writ large. • • •

Works Consulted

Alpers, Svetlana; Emily Apter, Carol Armstrong, Susan Buck-Morss, et. al. 1996. "Visual Culture Questionnaire." *October* 77:25-70.

Bakhtin, M. M., translation by Michael Holquist. 1981. *The Dialogic Imagination: Four Essays*. Austin: University of Texas Press.

Caillois, Roger. 1976. *Mitología del pulpo: ensayo sobre la lógica de lo imaginario*. Caracas: Monte Avila.

_____. 1984. "Mimicry and Legendary Psychasthenia." *October* 31:16-31.

Canetti, Elias. 1994. *Agony of Flies: Notes and Notations*. New York: Farrar, Straus and Giroux.

Clark, T. J. 1999. *Farewell to an Idea: Episodes from a History of Modernism*. New Haven: Yale University Press.

Cohen, Cora; Betsy Sussler. 1986. "Joan Mitchell (Interview)." *Bomb: A Quarterly on New Art, Writing, Theater and Film* (Fall):21023.

De Certeau, Michel. 1996. "Vocal Utopias: Glossolalias." *Representations* (56):29-47.

Elkins, James. 2003. *Visual Studies: A Skeptical Introduction*. London: Routledge.

Eshleman, Clayton, introduction by Eliot Weinberger. 1986. *The Name Encanyoned River: Selected Poems, 1960-1985*. Santa Barbara: Black Sparrow Press.

Eshleman, Clayton, edited by Caryl Eshleman, introduction by Paul Christensen. 1989. *Antiphonal Swing: Selected Prose 1962-1987*. 1st ed. Kingston, NY: McPherson.

Eshleman, Clayton. 1989. *Hotel Cro-Magnon*. Santa Rosa: Black Sparrow Press.

_____. 1994. *Under World Arrest*. Santa Rosa: Black Sparrow Press.

_____. 1998. *From Scratch*. Santa Rosa: Black Sparrow Press.

Eshleman, Clayton, foreword by Adrienne Rich. 2002. *Companion Spider: Essays*. Middletown, Conn.: Wesleyan University Press.

Eshleman, Clayton. 2003. *Juniper Fuse: Upper Paleolithic Imagination & the Construction of the Underworld*. Middletown, Conn.: Wesleyan University Press.

Iversen, Margaret. 1998. "Retrieving Warburg's Tradition," in *The Art of Art History: A Critical Anthology*, edited by D. Preziosi. Oxford: Oxford University Press.

Kofman, Sarah. 1988. *The Childhood of Art: An Interpretation of Freud's Aesthetics*, European Perspectives. New York: Columbia University Press.

Krauss, Rosalind. 1985. "Corpus Delecti." *October* 33:31-72.

Phillips, Adam. 2001. *Promises, Promises: Essays on Literature and Psychoanalysis*. New York: Basic Books.

Preziosi, Donald. 1989. *Rethinking Art History: Meditations on a Coy Science*. New Haven: Yale University Press.

_____. 1998. *The Art of Art History: A Critical Anthology*, Oxford History of Art. New York: Oxford University Press.

Tuma, Keith; Clayton Eshleman. 1996. "An Interview with Clayton Eshleman." *Contemporary Literature* 37 (2):179-206.

Warburg, Aby. 1998. "Images from the Region of the Pueblo Indians of North America." In *The Art of Art History: A Critical Anthology*, edited by D. Preziosi. New York: Oxford University Press.

Yakubinsky, Lev Petrovich; translated by Michael Eskin. 1997. "On Dialogic Speech." *PMLA* 112 (2):243-256.

RECIPROCAL DISTILLATIONS

WITCHERY

Realm of co-penetration, grotesque, affirmative,
I offer you what grows from my chest
in tumor-splendor, gnarled, polished, wet.

I protect you with all my navel blades,
my nipple nails, my kidney mirror—
dead mirror in which cloud fungus is trapped.

Steel pins puncture my thigh, belly and throat—
they enable me to pray with torturous force.

Mask reabsorbing the lost particulars of being,
mask replacing the bald human face with wilderness eyes,
mask sharing veins with its plant juice doubles,
mask whose interstices swarm with pupa.

If, over my tall blue pearled neck, I stare in terror, it is because
foxes have gotten inside me,
foxes are tearing apart my death.

Pitch-black head breaking out in red currants, in spikes, in blisters,
head a field sprouting buds, pebbles, studs,
head issuing a living waving horn,
head asleep, head replete, head whose dream matrix pustulates
the prayer of all things: to emerge, at once.

[Based on figures in
the Dapper Museum of African Art,
Paris]

You want to recover the original wholeness?

Re-enter chaos.

Kill your own profane existence.

Become a chocolate skull, wrapped in white silk, teeth sewn shut, sockets shell-stoppered.

The auroral instant prior to existence?

Death is a rite of passage, not an end.

In flight, an erection becomes the World Tree.

I am a crow perched in the foliage of my scattered skeleton.

From the mud under Satan's nails I have made a mound on which to rest.

An animal goes into a cave, re-emerges as a man.

The animal on the wall: earth cosmetics, cosmopathy, the make-up of inner space.

Spirits of the head.

Brow of unpolished wood.

My left eye a rouge of blood and sperm.

Eyeball: a rabbit balled-up in a cage.

A Mohawk hairjolt stiffened with soot.

The inner head, beat-up version of somebody else.

The whap in the jaw, slug of the male jaw, castrated bullet of the prognathus jaw.

Eye as moon crater.

The target of the eye.

Eye closed under a brain kindling geysers and splitting fontanels.

I am jawless with long, long ears, my throat extends to my eyes.

Spirits of the head.

Mustache of drool and loam.

Face of waves, of serpentine mobs.

Aviary face, eyrie of coons and owls.

Shore of the eye, quicksand of a look.

And then George Dyer—a spirit head if there ever was one—
  turned to show in profile
  a root-chopped, tusk dug continent,
  issue bandaged with eyelids and whiskers.

Dead Dyer with bumblebee lips.

Dyer with a snow cone blood picked nose.

Skull with nimbus of Germanic steel and gold.

Merry Xmas, Mr. Mayhem, I'm here to interrogate the nimbus of your
  lungs.

Here to enjewel your ribs with metal buttons, velvet flaps.

Head in rotary division, a single eye, mouth, and terrine of ears.

God has withdrawn into the Devil's Skull from which he fires spider
  filaments into the glory hole of mankind.

Within the face, Bosch working the pump: mouth slashes up into eye, eye
  bruises over, pickled garden of shredded amanitas and blind sables.

Pit of the face, cemetery pitted against chaos.

Brain as a tub of marrow filled with the diced hands of scientists.

Head of bone, of spirit, unbroken head.

Head destroyed and intact as a granite egg.

Lynched tongue-bunched neck invisible to the boys setting fire to its toes.

Fly of the human eye excreting as it broods.

Snowshoe of George Dyer's mouth planted in ice.

How much white can a head take? Can it assimilate supremacy, heaven?

Can it take on the reddened battlefield of man's pincer gaze at pluck with
  his brother?

Can I make the unsayable bark to verify that racial whitewash will never
  succeed in gating the community of souls?

Head on its hair body, homuncular head, alchemical gaze of a hair body
through which the putty of the face mills.

I have been studying the paintings of Francis Bacon since the early 1970s, and have written several poems based on notes taken while attending various exhibitions. In 1999, I purchased a copy of *Bacon: Portraits and Self-Portraits*. This collection focused on heads and reverberated with an exhibition I saw in Paris at the National Museum of African and Oceanic Arts of painted and decorated skulls from such places as Brazil, Peru, New Guinea, and Indonesia. Adorned with natural dyes, shells, vegetable fibers and clay, these tribal skulls vibrated with that mauve zone filled with two-way traffic between the living and the dead.

Since the Bacon heads often appear to be sites of violence, grotesque distortion, and psychological tumult, they connected with the decorated skulls, and because they were slashed and contoured with swirls of red, black, and especially white paint, they evoked a fantastic vision of the brain that is discussed by Weston LaBarre in *Muelos / A Stone Age Superstition about Sexuality* (a kind of 1984 addenda to his monumental study of the origins of religion, *The Ghost Dance*). Here is LaBarre's thesis:

> If bones are the framework of life, more specifically it is the semen-like marrow (*muelos*) in the bones that is believed to be the source of semen. The skull, as the bone enclosing the most plentiful *muelos*-marrow in the body (the brain), is therefore the major repository of the generative life-stuff or semen. Consciousness and life are the same stuff and thus have the same site. The idea seems bizarre and contrived to us only because we have forgotten the formative origins of our ideas. Yet, as later discussions will establish, the concept of brain-*muelos* as the source of semen is everywhere inherent in European thinking, as well as in that of societies elsewhere.
>
> (*Muelos*, p. 3)

Much of LaBarre's ethnographic information comes from areas on earth represented in the decorated skull show in Paris. Head-hunting for brain-eating purposes appears to run from the Neolithic up into the 20th century. This superstition accounts for aspects of human behavior that would otherwise remain mysterious or be misinterpreted. It not only, in part, explains cannibalism and head-hunting, but adolescent fellation, sodomy, and superstitions concerning ejaculation and women. Poets especially may be interested to know that among the New Guinea Asmat, in their origin myth of head-hunting, the decapitated skull can speak (as in the Orpheus legends) and hence can offer his name to an initiate.

*

Near the end of 1999, my wife Caryl was receiving physical therapy at the *Hands On Clinic* in Plymouth, Michigan, a half-hour drive from our home in Ypsilanti. I would drive her there and while she was receiving therapy would spend an hour or so at a nearby coffee shop, taking notes on my reading from the above-mentioned books (as well as a catalog from the decorated skull exhibition and an occult study by Kenneth Grant, *Outer Gateways*).

The point of this note taking was to create a kind of matrix of materials that I could then draw upon for a poem. There are around a dozen pages of notes leading up to the writing of "Spirits of the Head." As an example, here is one page of notes:

Alcheringa time
timeless time of the unconscious
immortal influence of our dead
  others upon us

Celtic head   solar symbol
  severed head
skulls facing west
heads that can exist in their
  own rights.
gilded head   holy vessel
(is the Grail a holified skull?)

raiding for slaves and human heads

skulls nailed into position on
  the lintel of the gateway
skulls at the bottom of storage pits

head literal seat of fertility
                (Celtic)

antlered Cernunnus
     animal fertility
—bring a skull home to get the babes!—
  springing of antlers from the life-stuff
  in the head

Earlier on the day that I wrote the poem (December 15, 1999), I took notes specifically on Bacon's portraits of his lover/model, George Dyer. What Bacon saw in male heads, Dyer's in particular, struck me as a clot of desire, rage, inspiration, and destruction, with asymmetrical planes exuding soul-stuff. The use of white evoked a combination of whipped cream and sperm, and thus the brain-*muelos* described by LaBarre. Bacon the head-hunter!

Dyer's Head

battered bolt
irregular screw (!)
chunk of rock
  semen spat
Cherokee topknot
head semen-spattered
  & blood-ripened,
raw, with blackened
  sperm sockets

head in a transparent
  body sock of blood and semen
soaked in soot

    on pink ground
      dog emerging from the whipping
kennel of the sperm-furred head

head flesh torqued as if on
  a rotary blade
oozing its life force, its
  muelos grubs

    *

I got to the question that opens the poem via pondering the decorated
skulls (in the exhibition catalog). If the head is charged with divinity, then
the taking of a venerated (or enemy) skull could be thought of as putting
its power on hold, of making its force ritually available for the living.

Line 4: description of one of the decorated skulls from the Marquesas Islands in Polynesia.

Line 9: plays off "the cosmic dive," probably the oldest known myth, of Upper Paleolithic antiquity. In its many versions, a creature dives to the bottom of the primordial seas to bring up a bit of mud from which the original land mass of the earth is formed. The lines in the poem extend this metaphor to a Cro-Magnon descent into a cave where, on the walls, with cave water and mineral pigments, humankind's earliest images were made.

After the poem's title is resounded, the following lines riff off fantasies of the head, with Bacon's portrait distortions just under the surface. With the mention of George Dyer, Bacon comes in directly.

"Merry Christmas, Mr. Mayhem" turns on the 1983 David Bowie film, "Merry Christmas, Mister Lawrence." The line is decorated, as it were, with 19th century decorated German skull images.

In the last strophe, "head on its hair body" comes from one of Bacon's images of the head of Isabel Rawsthorne, where her hanging hair is turned into little penguin-like flippers and an elfin body.

The end of the first draft was more elaborate than what I finally decided on. While I prefer the revision, the first version shows how I got there. After "in pluck with his brother," I originally wrote:

Can I release the animal of his
    face, this dog-spider, this cat-
    eel? Can the unsayable bark so
    as to verify that the racial
    whitewash will never totally succeed
    in gating the community of souls?
Soul head, squashed back against
    its matrix,
matrix of eye tires, phantomatic

swatch of hair, head on its
hair body, homuncular head,
alchemical gaze of a hairbody
through which the putty of the
face mills, reconstituting its
black flame ape-source hovering
existence's indentured antenna—

*

"Spirits of the Head" is a fantasia; while it proceeds to some extent via association, it is not "free association" or "automatic writing." When I was a kid, I had one kind of firecracker that did not explode, but issued a long curling smoking worm out of its ball. I think of poems like this as extending out of themselves, as if all the lines to come are packed, in nucleus, in the opening lines, or, in this case, in the title.

Under this parthenogenetic image is a compositional method that I developed while doing research on the origin of image-making in the Ice Age caves of southwestern France. Here I would like to quote from the Introduction to my book *Juniper Fuse: Upper Paleolithic Imagination & the Construction of the Underworld*:

> In the late 1970s, Alexander Marshack showed Caryl and me a photo of an incised ox rib from an Acheulean dig near Bordeaux. The astonishing thing was that between 200,000 and 300,000 years ago a hominid appears to have made a curving slash in the bone (referred to by Marshack as a "core meander"), and then to have placed this cutting instrument on the slash and made another curving cut (referred to as a "branch meander"). This act was repeated several times... Whoever made these "meanders" was, in a subliminal way, creating history (thinking

here of "history" in the Charles Olson derived sense of "istorin, to find out for oneself," in which I would put the stress on "out," or exit for the self). Taking a lead from the caves and the terms Marshack used, I attempted to find a way to branch out in my poetry while keeping a core at work within the meandering. I sought a focused movement forward through material that would keep open to associative side-tracks... Later, I read Anton Ehrenzweig's commentary, in *The Hidden Order of Art*, on the relation of the maze to the creative search, and realized that my approach to core and branch meandering was a way of schematizing the labyrinth I entered when I started to work on a poem.

So, with "head" as its "core," "Spirits of the Head" puts out "branch meanders" as it works its way along, such as "the World Tree," "Satan's nails," "Mr. Mayhem," and "Bosch working the pump." I seek in each of these lines to present material that a reader could not have anticipated, but which, when it occurs, seems uncommon-sensically relevant, and a stud in the poem's overall intended coherence.

For over 50 years Leon Golub has plunged through blood marshes,
cutting through the daymare of his era, translating
classic chaos, conceiving the homuncular man of history.
By removing the 20th century zero of history in museums from the
  scales,
he has rebalanced them with *art as social meaning.*
Golub as man self-revealed on his ground,
grounded as in flamenco, the work pushed
down, into post-Whitmanian nuclear grass,
no longer a lode of white-haired mothers,
but a depository for Angola land-mines. It is the rush of man
out of the umbilicus forever bombing,
it is the fire, the spurt of lamb, at the edge of everyone's sight.

Earth, does your subjectility still have amnion?
Is finding one's spot still the key revision of fetal drift?
A given paradise is no more.
Memory, working with psyche, can argue, can reveal.
Golub's figures are shadowed with lost ground.
We know where man is when we look at these paintings.
We see a range of acrid flavors,
out of Vietnam with a hint of the awful, striped with
tribal hybridity, woman as gate, woman as beautiful sphinx—

Golub now works in blackness
projecting Día de Muertos stigmata through
the oil slicks of American culture,
fragments of the elderly Prometheus, the merc-headed dog caught in blue

street light,
the interior rims of America, neon-stung slums where
Blacks and Chicanos crouch in the combustion zone of a voodoo particle
   flow.
Our eyes are steined with Clinton
whose guts must look like a Boschian symphony.
Wake up, daddy bones,
nothing is not bad. Nothing is the ultimate ground.

I construct a skull for Leon,
place it in the Borneo men's house at 71st and Broadway,
a cowrie shell for each socket.
I caress his skull top with gutta percha,
making crosses and Nixon cartoons in the rubbery resin,
then I drape this skull in dreadlocks
and elongate it back into Merovingian time.
Surely Leon Golub deserves that depth.

[10 December 2000]

Corot, 1870

Leaves,   masses of milling
   disintegrating moths

Wildflowers as brightly-colored fleas

Speck-enthralled earth encaved by shadow waves

A piece of watery dark grows in the woods
liquidating the struts of matter

   Buried in shadow
the day-lit world. A cow wades a lake
as if regarding the boy fishing,
as if alive. Corot's eventide at
      high noon

            In her up-
               gathered pale rose gown,
      a young woman offers a wildflower-filled
               womb urn to
               khaki leaf fumes

Buried in shadow
"The springtime of life"

Virgin in a fire storm of cherries

How nature umbilically

divides,
multiplies out,   moss plush blue marsh,
        spider webbed creek glass

Anything perceived, implicit armature

        Sky tight
absence-mangered woods

                You are dead. Dream now,
drift into this castle-bordering lake's black sustinence

Are we but animations of shadow glades,
shadow figments
seamless to each,
animated by
    shadow-static drives?

As the syrup shade comes up in you, hold high
the momentary tambourine
    —O my monstrance,
    my aura, seized and sounded!

                    [for Bob Holkeboer & Paola Valsania]

There is in Michaux an emergent face/non-face always in formation. Call it "face before birth." Call it our thingness making faces. Call it tree bole or toadstool spirits, *anima mundi* snout, awash in ephemerality, anti-anatomical, the mask of absence, watercolor by a blind child, half-disintegrated faces of souls in Hades pressing about the painter Ulysses-Michaux as, over his blood trench of ink, he converses with his hermaphroditic muse...

Ink beings spear themselves into rupturing elfin thumbs.

The doubles enrubble, cobble ruins, gobble gobble, aerial brains.

Zigzagging corpuscles surprised by a bacterial whinny.

Reintegration at the cost of re-entry.

Black sand dense on white ground. Mites. Mites in mitosis. Mitochondria. Miscible mites. Mitomitosalchondrialmaze.

A gangrenous, thousand-windowed penile haze.

Backed by scarlet maggots, by teeny-weenies, by fetal corn flakes.

A glacial stadium enraged by a torii invagination.

Clothespins cutting up with squidy lattices, no, phosphenic lesions, yes, cruciliquinixies.

Once razed, the mind's hive releases mastodontal honey.

Mescalinian nets through which infant marmalade englobes.

I am free in Michaux, free to be coccolithic, a gas candy bar, whatever...

Better: everwhat. What forever what.

Being unbound. Unbound being bonded.

Ever in the state of *what!*

Everwhat sun. Everwhat dust.

A powder of points. Veil

pulled back, the revelation is lithic velum.

A line encounters a line, evades a line.

A line waits, hopes, a line rethinks a face.

Ant-high lines. Ant-visibles streaming through lines.

A melodic line crosses twenty stratigraphic fractures.

A line germinates. Martyr-laughable lines.

Lines gaslighting lines. Lines budding on a dune.

A dream of paradise: lines in conversation with their liminal selves.

The linen of lines, worn, lineage of proliferating life lanes.

The Minotaur as a horned line.

Bitter combat at the center of a line.

What is the center of a line?

Where the whatever folds, becomes everwhat.

Ramose, lachrymose hollow of lines, sisters of stain.

Stains immaculate in their sordid, humid bellies.

Jonah-Michaux in the moray mescaline belly.

Aimé Césaire's "stiff wine of moray eels," overboard cast slaves harvested
by morays.

Dry furnace of a landscape. Stampeding tacks, lassoed by Jesus, lassoed
by Sartre.

The scolopendra line. The cockchafer line.

Lines milling insectile to their rodent spoils.

The Last Judgment performed by worms.

The tick faces in gorilla traces.

Lines in reason's glare seething with kettle life.

Nematodes in round dance on a hyena vagina.

Facing Darger, 34 floors below—
can I reach his station? The Darger Abyss,
below the subconscious, in Tartarus,
where giants are bound to little girls?
With what are the Titans bound?
The anguish of one's mother as a little girl enslaved?
Darger washed hospital basins, cleaned up mess.
Was he tied up at The Lincoln Asylum for Feeble-Minded Children
when he was 12? What happened to Darger?
Why was Darger Darger? He escaped across a river, 1909.
"The farm," I read, was a concentration camp of sorts,
masturbators and kickers tied up, trussed on the floor in their own feces.
His mother dead from puerperal septicima when he was 4
died giving birth to Henry's sister immediately given up for adoption.
Raised by his father, a crippled tailor, until 8.
What Darger made of his empty basin is remarkable,
test of a human being unwilling to die,
a nothing man who scratched out of trash something.
Civil War = Internal War = God vs. Man.
The slavery man is to himself, pitiful man infantile to God.
The societal closes over. Why speak to those whose hearts wear witch
    hats?
Grim 1912 Chicago. Moonflake streets.
Collections of newspaper cartoons pasted in bulging volumes,
bits of string tied into 500 balls.
Keep the heart away from the cleaver,
keep the cleaver bared to Bad Men, big-hatted guys
he had torturing naked girls. In Darger's dream

the soldiers never touch the girls, they strangle them, disembowel them,
but do not touch them. The girls do not touch themselves.
They have cartoon penises, with muff-like balls.
They are immortal. Most cannot speak.

"It's the prank of the whole earth
against whoever has balls in his cunt," wrote Antonin Artaud,
who likewise ejaculated "daughters of the heart, to be born."
Here is an Artaud/Darger daughter-braid:

> Yvonne
> > Hansonia
> Caterine
> > Catherine
> Neneka
> > Angeline
> Cécile
> > General Vivian
> Ana
> > Violet
> Little Anie
> > Jennie
> Colette
> > Gertrude

At the intersection of Darger and Artaud,
there's a Frida Kahlo bus accident hourly.
Armored spirits ram a daughter-filled vessel
spraying heads and limbs into psychic containers—

> "Everything must be arranged
>   to a hair
> in a fulminating
>   order"

Poor Darger, the poorest of the 20th century tribe of imaginal founders;
at mass in strait-rosary 4 times daily,
cleaning up hospital waste for 50 years
(his one friend moved away)
sleeping upright in a chair at 851 Webster Avenue
(his cot looked like Charles Olson's worktable),
a library of children's books and hymnals
grubbed out of trash cans or bought for pennies.
Caryl and I made a list of his library
when we visited his room in 1997:

13 Oz volumes   9 Dickens volumes
Making the Weather   Sources of Volcanic Energy
Autumn Leaves   Trini The Little Strawberry Girl
Tisa A Little Alpine Waif   The Best of Friends
Rinkitink   A Little Maid Of Nantucket
Heidi Grows Up   The Lost Princess
The Patchwork Girl   Meet The Bobsey Twins
The Bobsey Twins Camping Out   The Kitten's Secret
Defending His Flag Or A Boy In Blue & A Boy In Gray
Lorraine And The Little People Of The Ocean
The Revolt Of The Angels   Kidnapped
Official Guide Book (World's Fair, 1934)
Wheelers' Graded Readers, 2 volumes
Sweethearts Unmet   The Great Chicago Fire

The Banner Boy Scouts Snowbound   Rare Old Chums
The Cheery Scarecrow   St. Basil's Hymnal
Christian Brothers Hymnbook   Fun With Decals
Spirit Of The Blessed Cure Of Arts   Rosemary
The House Of 1000 Candles   Little Red Riding Hood
Mathematics For Common Schools   Peter Pan
A Shirley Temple Story Book   The Life of Christ
Dion Quintuplets "Going On Three"   The Rose Child
The Atlas "Biology"   Andersen's Fairy Tales
Blind Agnesse   The School Of Jesus Crucified
Jo The Little Machinist   The Little Christmas Shoe
Catechism Of Christian Doctrine   Grimm's Fairy Tales
My Child Lives (Consoling Thoughts of Bereaved Parents)
Sick-A-Bed Sally   A Guide To The Franciscan Monastery
Don Quixote   Condemned To Devil's Island

Fleas with tyke faces crawl 5'3" Darger.
To adopt? That too denied me?
I am Chicago Weather, Hendro Darger the Volcanologist,
author of a 15,000 page novel, Pepto-Bismol bottle collector,
I rescue crucifixes from trash cans,
my eyeglasses held together by tape,
wallet tied to shoestring attached to belt loop.
Jesus, are you a little girl? Jesus, am I in
your body? Nail-wracked Jesus,
        am I your daughter
           self?

*

Darger is too absolute to tinker with,
he's a first and last man,

a man without middle (most artists are
bunched in passage, they periscope and

they retract). I go to Darger to
clear my life of life's mid-way.

Darger is sympathetic
because he chose to move at all.

He could have jammed his head into a toilet.
He chose not to, chose to

cosmogonize a burr
lodged in his heart.

Darger in his child zoo, testing liberation.
Darger as a child zoo, refusing liberation.

No matter how many carnivores he releases,
the Vivian Girls are trillion in a field.

    *

Northrop Frye, reading Blake's *Thel*:

"nothing achieves reality without going through physical existence, the
descent must be made. The failure to make it is the theme of *The Book of
Thel*. Thel is an imaginative seed: she could be any form of embryonic life,

and the tragedy could be anything from a miscarriage to a lost vision... being an embryo in the world of the unborn, Thel longs to be of 'use,' that is, to develop her potential life into an actual one and hence come into our world of Generation... But, hearing the groans of a fallen world tormented in its prison, she becomes terrified and escapes back to the unborn world... a world of dissolving and arbitrary fantasy, a looking-glass world of talking flowers... *The Book of Thel* thus represents the failure to take the state of innocence into the state of experience... in Thel's infertile world everything is exquisite and harmless... Thel's canvas is decorated with lambs and lilies."

So, the Darger girls are frozen seeds, stripped of garment, to show their seed nature. They do not move imaginatively, but pout, pose, or flee the head-charged Glandelinian femaleless males. The girls repopulate endlessly, each a mirror of the other (they pop up as exact duplicates or in series). Where they should be concave, they are convex, un-enterable, which means they are unable to enter experience. By giving them penises, Darger makes invasion impossible. The girls' unborn boyfriends are the saintly Blengiglomenean Serpents, with long wavy tails. While they do shoot fluid into the girls (which the latter appear to like, and which makes them immortal), this only confirms that the two mix on a sperm and egg level, a level in Darger which never produces babies.

*

Galleries of the defiled, undefiled in Darger's dream,
millions he can commemorate and save,
bland blazing paradox, terrible sandwich of eternity,
the dead behind, the here static.
These commercial images of children—
Coppertone Lotion sold by a child's panties being

tugged by a doggy, images of tots used to sell children clothes
or cigarettes, via smoking adults towering over—
Darger stripped them, mummies are more immediate,
Darger is more savage, more blank.
Do his 300 scrolls contain the paradise of the unlived,
the "early departed"? It matters immensely
that Darger's mother died when he was 4,
giving birth to a sister he never saw.
Little girls, cute absences in repetitional grids—
I am ashamed to identify them: yellow hair, in orange collar,
yellow dress, stands beside brown hair, arms crossed
over tummy, in red play suit, red anklets, before
brown and red ball, next to yellow hair in orange collar,
yellow dress, hands behind her—
are these the forepleasures of childhood
as death manipulates budding energies to stain each into each?
Darger is the remainder of the huge absence I felt as a child,
"staring at a corner for hours," my mother told Caryl,
"he was such a good boy." But oh, my childhood,
for all of its ills, was redolent with sap compared to Henry's.
His naked girls are without pathos, and—they are totally pathetic,
unborn, reflecting neither forward nor backward.
Coppertone cutie is stripped not only of her panties
but of her pseudo-persona. "She" is the girl who never is,
multiplied as if through the fly-eyed lens of God.
Darger had no idea—or did he?—that he was creating a pantheon.
We peer at it in the American Museum of Folk Art,
goodness, what is on that man's mind?
Moral mayhem, amigo, girls tinier than pink flowers,
leaping ram-headed fairies, fashion ads
stripped of their null frivolity become

girl negatives, crucified en mass or oddly screaming,
neck-twisted, in a collage margin.
Is paradise the absence of adults?
The absence of experience, its fallow, planted perpendiculars?
Can paradise possibly *be* if we preclude experience?
Darger opens up a worm vista on paradise—
his art is the negation of an active paradise,
one of imagination, one shamans zoom into, a state
unobtainable through political or anatomical means.
Darger rubs our faces in the gleet of the impossibility of paradise.
Good for you, Henry, stunted and friendless,
thanks for rubbing our commodity-drugged mugs through
these image-angel-less anti-ikons. But there are so many
crossword bunnies in the woods, so much jigsaw shadow—
did Darger ever know where he was? Possibly,
but only in the grand orality of his red weather,
tourbillions of girl necks whistling through what flavored his life, natal
   tornado.
Comic strip valley aswarm with cradle-shaped rangers.
Radiant sweetness shotgun emptied into dot-eyed zombies.

An andesite, chubby Ganesha, in lotus
position with adz-shaped ears and

rubble cap of petrified worms.
In one palm, a broken tusk

stylus—the other palm holds an inkwell
into which his trunk is dipped.

Is that brain ink he's pumping out?
Parthenogenetic

uroboros. Take a self-subtracted
art from me. Feed your adder.

You are mist.

The contours of certain cave walls invite engagement.
Hosts in the wall, bald, convex,
hold vigil over mental drift. To populate
the moonscape of a wall. To draw in lit craters
the squirm and reel of incarnate trial.
Their bellies hang low, their shoulders
rise and sink like pistons, each step is placed
soundlessly. *Panthera spelea*. Larger than
the African lion. Larger even
than the Amur tiger. Maneless. Craning forward.
Cheeks bulging. Heads telescoping out of heads.
Eyes dilated. Knowingly, lovingly rendered.
Deftly shaded. Bone structure and depth.
Some are sheer outline, limestone showing through.
73 in all. One with blubber lips evokes
a hominid cartoon. The monster of God sensed
as manivore. Deity as predator. Jehovah's foreskins.
Zeus Lykaios. Behind sacralized violence,
the trauma of being hunted, and eaten. Check this:
animal holocaust in the late Ice Age
corresponds with the rise of war.
Cowl of the master dark,
its red breath heading west
toward a tilting vertical
"totem" of bison heads, spitted
like big furry bugs. Baby mammoth with
wheel feet. Hoofs seen from below? Full moons?
Body shaded smoky tan. Over it

a massive bison emerging from a fissure.
Two turned-toward-us bison heads,
one on lion haunch, one on lion shoulder.
Carnivore tattoos. Targets. Earliest body decor.
Drink to me only with thine
fangs. Energy I would induct. In dank
scrape light, as if Arshile Gorky
traced his life dark as lion space,
or Hans Bellmer, his erotic unending line
alive with orgasm's blocked flue.
Enkidu. Humbaba. Teelget. Hercules at Nemea.
Grendel "bit into his bone-lappings,
bolted down his blood
and gorged on him in lumps, leaving his body
utterly lifeless, eaten up
hand and foot." Astarte on lion back.
Artemis with a bull scrotum necklace.
Rhino with 8 oversized curving parallel horns,
as if drawn by Marcel Duchamp.
Rhino Descending a Lion Stare.
Stuttering horns. River pour of meated miles,
horns trestling dawn as red deer foam through.
See-saw of rhino bodies. "Central stripes"
make them look like "armored" Indian rhinos.
Sketchbook of this wall. Started, thwarted.
Body parts in fugal maze. Sacrificial diagram.
Palimpsest of beasts and humans. No finish.
But finish is near. As I stand on this aluminum ramp,
a CEO is stretching his eyeball around the planet
like an interstellar Santa, bag full and off to Saturn.

At the Kerlescan megalithic alignments

      the opened   loaded
            field

Stegosaurian plates
welted with lichen, granular
   saffron wounds

        I write
from the "lectern" of one
piece of Car, Ker, the Carmenta
    scattered

Kali Ma our Kauri, the cowrie did it, or was it Carya,
   the walnut-tree?
Kerlescan, you are not only dedicated to Ker, but to Kore,
   Q're, Car-Dia, Cerdo, Carna,
your progeny are carnivals, charms, karma, cherubs,
the kernel thanks you, charity is born,
because of you we have cereal, Ceres, we are carnal,
close kindred, there are cardinal points, cairns, the kern
   out of which the grain god spiked

At times these stones converge into a cromlech
to accommodate an animal band: the lion is seated
sawing away at his zebra harp, the bull is covering
his Leda-drum, the snake is playing the human spine

as if it were a chakra clarinet—

KA,

the curl of infant lip, fern drifting onto a sleeping
    dragon's out-lapped tongue,

stand

knee-deep in the flamy plush of this tongue,
ka becomes ka-r, currr, open ka seeking closure.
At the end, his vehicle lost, Olson moaned:

"my wife   my car..."

These tall stones wear
on their granite the menstrual stains of dusk—
as the moon conceals herself forth, they seem to push on,
toward the ark of etymologies...

I've swallowed the millstone of my father, no special feat,
the trick is to reimagine him, to think of him as a bean,
to go with the grinding, Car, nut nymph or Carytid?
Caer Sidin, the top of the pestle is in the Corona Borealis,
Caer Arianrhod, the Cretan wife of Dionysus

To be human is to be stretched between one's tomb, her names,
    and one's star,
part of me is a prisoner in Caer Sidin, the animal mortar,
I am the Beast trying to move Beauty through
    the sorgum of my eyes,

glint of Caer Arianrhod

in my iris implosions, distant Caer Arianrhod,

crown of the North Wind

As a poet my *cor*, my heart, is under Cerridwen,

I am of cerdd, grain and the inspired arts,
the feast of lady Carnea is June 1, my birth and wrath day.
As a *cerdo*, a craftsman, I have eaten *cerdo*, pig,
my character goes back to *carato*, from *qirat*, bean, to Carnea:
    pig meat and beans.
I have swallowed my father, his attempt to enwomb and to be reborn,
I raise my *keras*, horns, cuckolded by the power of Charybdis—
as a door I am the son of Cardea, from *cardo*, hinge,

                                by these forces

  am I permeated,

    anima is *pneuma*, the soul a storied fart.

                             [In memory of Paul Blackburn]

He shook the Counter-Reformation
decorum out of these *tableau vivants*,
eliminating from painting
saccharin distortion and ecclesiastic agit-prop.
If by "the human" we mean actual lives
kicking up dust as they speed toward us
shattering idealistic frames,
then Caravaggio, like Vallejo's *Human Poems*,
produced human paintings.
A young whore in red dress dumped on a simple bed:
"The Death of the Virgin."
The painting refuses the porcelain vagina.
There is no Jesus appearance, just Carmelite men,
convulsed, confused. Whore or virgin, she is laid out,
feet bare, arms and hands dangling
carnivorous, red shadow. The canopy bucks, collapses,
stung through by sin and atonement—
Caravaggio could not completely
slip the Christian corset.
He tore it, revealed its sweated inner lining.
In the destroyed "Resurrection"
it is said that he depicted Christ as
an emaciated convict climbing out of a pit.
What was this painter's engine?
What does his strong room look like?
The 1602 "John the Baptist in the Wilderness"
(with a gorgeous, naked "Baptist" pulling his ram to him,
a gesture rich with animal coitus),

and the "Victorious Cupid" (a naked fuck-boy with wings,
offering himself joyously to the viewer)
would not have been realized by a heterosexual painter.
He painted the Baptist eight or nine times,
at first using Biblical trappings to be able to work with
adolescent flesh. The story of someone
living on locusts and wild honey,
shaman-like with his lamb or ram familiar,
a moral loudmouth, perfect grist for
a despot's mill, is of little concern.
These attributes only register on Malta,
site of Caravaggio's second undoing, 1607.
He arrives with a capital ban on him (for the accidental
killing of Ranuccio Tomassoni who
provoked him over a small debt), meaning:
anyone can sever his head and present it to a judge
for a reward anywhere under Papal jurisdiction.
With the image of the severed head,
we open his strong room. There is the 1597 "Medusa,"
with a shocked, young Caravaggian face,
the 1599 "Judith and Holofernes" jetting blood
as the repulsed but turned on Judith
saws through the neck bone (the fact that the model
for Judith is a 17-year-old whore transforms
the Biblical setting into a brothel).
There are three "Davids with the Head of Goliath,"
the finest of which, done in 1609 or 1610
after the painter's face had been slashed outside
a Naples' tavern, depicts a pained, even sorrowing, David
holding out the head of—Caravaggio!
David withdraws, with his other arm,

his sword from his crotch. Implication:
the beheading of Goliath/Caravaggio is David's self-castration,
or, the Goliath/Caravaggio head is David's phallus.
Tomassoni bled to death from a sword-nicked penis.

On Malta, he paints "The Beheading of Saint John the Baptist"
as payment for becoming a Knight of Obedience.
Prison yard dark, 17th century Valletta.
Night in brownish-black settles through,
just enough rakes of light to see, in silence,
what men robotically visit on each other.
The Baptist lamb-trussed on the dirt,
neck partially slit. The executioner,
gripping a fistful of long Baptist hair,
yanks the head toward us, as, with his right hand,
he pulls a small knife from his leather belt sheath.
His rigid left arm is vertical architecture—
in the deltoids, triceps, radial forearm muscles,
contoured with amber shadow, ivory light,
I sense a sculptural Last Judgment
(it is as if the Ivory Tower rose from the ground of
the Baptist's "rape"). The executioner's
white bloomer folds have been painted so that
between his legs a phallic loop dangles,
inches over the Baptist's red cloak-covered rump.
Under this cloak: his lamb pelt,
the two forked legs of which jut out
as if from his groin. They are vulva-evocative.
The castrational humiliation of beheading
underscored by implicit buggery.
Baptist as catamite. Under the blood

oozing from the cut neck Caravaggio has
—the one time in his life—
signed: "f michelAn," directly from the blood blob.
In what spirit does the painter sign?
"f" = "fra," brother—and as a man,
condemned to duplicate the Baptist's fate—
and as a martyr to his own cause
which is, in the spirit of Herodian denunciation,
to tell the visual truth, to penitentially argue,
as an artist, the glacial contradiction between
transcendental hope and squalid reality.

After 1608, along with the Goliath/Caravaggio head,
there are two "Salomés with the Baptist's Head,"
including the executioner and the old woman witness
who, like a compressed Greek chorus,
holds her own "head oh head oh head don't leave me now!"
over the Malta beheading. The three float
as partially bodied heads in inky blackness about
the head-charged platter. The heads of Salomé and granny
implicitly share the same torso
as if making up a whole. Given Caravaggio's
fixation on the Baptist and Goliath,
with the signature and the painter's ruined face,
a dyadic Caravaggio is evoked,
a Baptist-Goliath, two heads sprouting off
the same severed neck, or
off the same severed erection
—while there are soft penises in the oeuvre,
there are no erections, so erection may be
the undepictable "thing," in Vallejo's words,

Caravaggio's "dreadful thing thing,"
generating the decapitational obsession.
Neck as erection, stem connecting
root to bloom, yes, but also the demonic link between
damnation-pocked head and runaway body,
this head that cannot really "lose itself"
as long as the neck yokes.

Four months after becoming a Knight,
Caravaggio is said to have been thrown into
the Fort Sant'Angelo oubliette,
to have gotten out of this eleven-foot-deep "hole,"
and to have sailed to Syracuse. There is
no record of his misdeed or crime on Malta,
nor how he was able to escape the "hole"
or who arranged his successful flight.
Peter Robb conjectures that the painter got caught
with one of the pages that his sponsor had
imported into unruly Valletta.
"Sex with a page would have been the ultimate outrage."
So they whisked Caravaggio out of there,
stripped him of his Knighthood (he left the island
without permission), leaving him to his own devices.

One of his Maltese paintings is a portrait of his sponsor,
Adolf de Wignacourt, Grand Master.
Next to Wignacourt in full armor is a page in red hose
looking directly at the painter (as very few subjects do),
holding Wignacourt's large red-plumed helmet.
If one takes the Goliath/Caravaggio head from David's grasp,
and superimposes it over the Grand Master's helmet,

Robb's conjecture is visualized. Grand Master
(surely the profoundly offended in this scenario),
delectable page, and Caravaggio as the Goliath-to-be,
a kind of *ménage à trois*. The unacknowledged
Maltese crime is, in its own way,
duplicated in July 1610. Caravaggio has disappeared,
his body is never found, all the official
reports of his demise make no sense.
Robb thinks he was murdered, probably by
people associated with the family of the man
he had killed. Martyrdom and salvation
are packed into the double Caravaggio head.
His paintings show, in compressed form,
a new self, released from Scholastic rote,
cloaked in Venetian red. Behind it:
desire for revelation, not of a transcendental ilk,
but of the soul made monstrous. Out of this full showing,
the true life of humanity—the poor, the tortured,
the saintly, the common, mother and child—may assemble.
Caravaggio gyrates on in me. I have,
in my stomach, some of his hermetic lantern shards,
undigestible martyrdom/salvation.

RADIX

Improvisations for Khaled Al-Saa'i

Language breaks forth with alphabet demons,
the *divs* and *devas* whose spiral
nebular orgasms generated wheeling uncials,
cursive minuscules. Ah the tongue wars
in Cro-Magnon night talk, the pain of firewood
felt by an erect iris voiced
as vowels like aimless planets coursing
the consonantal ink of libido carving outward.
Language starts up below as a root
discontent—as a human sphinx
peers out of a maned cave,
a queen force generates bags of letter fodder
becoming the breasts of masked amoebic engineers!

Al-Saa'i sees nature as intelligible word lore mortal scored rims
or rhymes, a lingo ribbonesque with inner din
(questers sounding themselves
off stone in a darkness sparkling with
ghoul-infested whirligigs, Sheela-na-gigs, the jig of the mind
in torque about the bud of self).

Through Al-Saa'i's swervy, granular latticeworks
I see the world of the *Shah-nameh*. Transport to rocks
blushing with vegetation, peonies swelling
with crimson joy, leafless twigs seething with bio-remorse,
the oyster-fresh eyes of rocks, rocks
pecking their way out of their shells—
then I return to Al-Saa'i's calligraphic airs

in which light can be sensed praying,
I enter its minty densities, its reptilinear interlocking sway,
its alpha radiant omega drone. I witness the caravan departure of
a great octopus rising from the waves,
transforming the tentacle water shudder into
a lacework of letter flavor cometary clover!

White flowers scissor-billowing the hemlock.

Where you begin is
a line tossed out, to catch on its own slant.
Your second move? Another line
punning across the first, as when one word
mounts another. Fishing the void, seeing if something
tugs back, and if not? The vexation of starting over
while keeping what was done.
Little Lulu's chair. A strip of chicken. What do
these shapes signify? A gesture, a gravid
reeling out. As if the lines were emerging from you,
spurting from many nipples.

How say this stroke works
but that does not? What is broken advances,
pillowed by what will not yield:
a thought drinking its shadow.

Loss looms. The loom hums.
An image is forming, a centripetal centrifuge
gusting erratic webs in the cream. Which peaks
and scrams,
almost, for nothing ever entirely leaves.
What seems to disappear has only camouflaged itself
as godfill.
Something has entered the composition that is alien to it.
I think of the Nephila
in her golden web unaware

hatched wasp larvae are feeding on her blood.
A blow-up of her midgut reveals
the septic aviary. Cross-outs galore
reassemble as
a burning lamb!
The painting as an enraged lamb!
In what neuron lode of your brain did rapture
misfire as rape?
                              To somehow get
the blood of the world in, the shed blood, the blood you cannot
see, or even know about, but know is shed.
Is this carmine or massacre red?
Is this chockablock knot
the scene of a crime, or quarried depth,
the two dimensional
clotting in psyche as a lioness crossing
the blood stream of your? of my? heart—and do I
want my heart to be played by
an auburn carnivore emotion,
or, by a caterpillar band? Oh so much of you is here,
just in swaying drip lines, nematocystic tentacles...

You leave before you arrive, you arrive
without having come. But is this not the spring of
self-invention? Of moving out an all,
unconfined by figure or representation, a presence
sea-urchin erect with menstruation, drunkenness,
fucking, friendship! All of which are sensed and hived below
our meeting ground, internal aviation,
our dog fight in the clouds! zooming under you,
then you pepper me from behind, in flames I go down

through a blob of vermilion and a swath of no,
entangled in the ur-done, the undone, the never to be
is pulling something from me,
a memory tugged out of its carapace.

As you aged, the spider milk level lowered,
lifting into view a branchwork in staccato detour,
the casserole of a capillary thatch,
moulting
switchbacks, hemlock breakthrough become
your linden in slow explosion, as if the maw of the universe
had opened, pandoric, and Hope
had triumphed, consuming all her sister ills.

The periscope's mirror now a kaleidoscopic exit into
yellow tormentil stars, blue
dove-gray milkwort sprays,
lilac marsh violets, a field unfolding,
chopped turbulence, crocked,
eternally vernal, your friend Gisèle's
girlhood valley, explored only by those who knew
the location of the secret entrance, this
flushed paradise forth! Packed anagrammatic
closure, blue
loaded with black, affirmation
with hell in tow, azure ribbed with struts of
incorporated erasure. Vincent's crows,
wrung out black propellers lathing
corn trampled into ochre lightning.

Whose death mask is being molded with
these rampant arctotheric clouds?

How divine the state of the union in
the entrails of
Daisy Mae?

Bill, you are a master
vacuum, an ethereal
mulberry bay. In Hiroshige's
paradisal shade
                    I imagine you
cutting a wood block under a plum tree,
            listening to Bud Powell.

"Printing is a controlled burst of furious energy, more on the side of
finesse than ham-fisted strength. All important are the first zig-zag motions,
pushing the paper down on the colored block, that gets most of the job
done—at the right pressure with the right baren, of course."
                    Miraculous
Japanese American chiasma.
Under it: a blackened German Expressionist grill,
like watching a man make ice cream
over flames,
        but yours *held*,
a miracle of aerial
    tensions.
            Blue Monument,
torii spread across three panels, knobbed,
rubbly, the rigor of
withstanding tempest,   and prayer.

    Texture of Kyoto temple walls,
slate floors,   in your prints their surface is fragmented,
one looks into rocky ochre mural anatomy,   not the Buddha,
but emanational architecture,

or *Flowers*

from **Brother Stones**
Clayton Eshleman / Poet
William Paden / Printmaker
Kyoto 1968
A Caterpillar Book

Hooded women
before a green hill.
Mixed in the hill
red sky.
        Ancestors by roadside
never seen in these cities.

I am either a friend of myself
or nothing.

    *

Bloomington, 1957: In a poker game, I won $20 from someone who said, "I don't have the money, here, take this painting." Busts of a man and a woman, the loser having punched a hole in the guy's lips, stuck in a cigarette. Bottom right corner: "W. Paden." I asked around. Someone said you were living down on the square, having just been released from a hospital. I knocked. We became friends. You gave me the New Directions *20th Century Latin American Poetry* (1944), in which I discovered Pablo Neruda and César Vallejo. Later, someone else said you were hospitalized because you had tried to kill yourself in New York City.

Mike Armstrong, in Cincinnati, once told me he pulled you away from a Lower East Side roof edge. If he knew what was eating you, he never told me. Nor did you.

    *

Lodged in my mind, now,
the animal miles in your eyes,
beached sea lion, half-propped in hospital gown.

A little quiet, please, my friend is
dying here. Open the window, elope him
quickly to the void. No, wait,
he wants to run his full incarnation,
a gauntlet no one can trace.

Or better, some noise. What is the point of savior
if crocodiles show more respect? After is
nowhere, the realm some artists
kiss. Why has a tube been forced between his lips?
Because he is in migration? O
blow through him what he has achieved!

      *

Born four years after you, a dozen blocks north,
I'm wandering an Indianapolis   out of time.
Everywhere: the lack of imagination,   miasmatic
church churn. How did we ever escape this whirlpool
racist grip of spiritual ennui?   Well, we didn't—
    out of a nullity we arched into art, seeking an inner face,
    a mask within.
                 We carried within us
the shame of contradicting ourselves, being for and
against self...
              It is as if I still drag behind me
—like some horrible extension of my own waste—

the things and activities that made no sense,
the maze of tracks on which my parents robotized,
not knowing how to live,   truly alone
with others,   trying to figure out how to say what?
and when?...
                    I am back in the hospital now
with you, with a huge teardrop
embroidered on your gown,
Fiat Lux,   the sorrow of
light perforating
shadow, the original
impulse of creation
a teardrop, a curved vessel

                *

A black slash of earth unbars height and depth
   solar pink infests
a granite sea's mottled maroon vein-work,
        of us,   of the *hanga* maker's
                    hand

The sky   dilates with departure
mountain layers drift   cloud shale   higher
            the light of heaven
                    whitens why...

Sunset—a masterpiece.   Did you believe that it was pointless to try
to sell your work? That *moku hanga* could be of no interest to
the American art world? Or did you believe, with Emily Dickinson,
    Publication is the Auction

Of the Mind of Man?
Why did you wait a year to deal with it
after finding out you had lung and esophageal cancer?

*

Kyoto, 1963: to get you out of NYC where it appeared you were destroying
yourself ("my hair is so filthy no barber will cut it" you wrote me), I sent
you a boat ticket for Japan. You stayed with Barbara and me for a month,
then moved into a modest former *ryokan* south of Seikanji monastery. We
introduced you to Yoshiko Isa, who moved in with you. One afternoon
she called and invited us to a party. We were busy. She called back, and
asked if we might be free the following week. We were, but we also thought
it strange that she would change the party just for us. It turned out the
"party" was being held in a temple, maybe 200 people were there, mostly
Yoshiko's relatives. As I wandered through the crowd I kept hearing the
word *kekkon*. You spoke no Japanese at this point. I pulled you into a
john and said: "do you realize this is your marriage party?" "No," you
responded, and then grinned, "well, why not?"

*

All of your Expressionist paintings have disappeared,
except the two you gave me, in 1968,
we had to take a window out of my loft, when you sold the rest,
maybe seventy canvases? for a pittance, to John Upham
(who has also disappeared)...

We had one fight, in nearly 50 years of friendship
—over Leon Golub, in the late 1980s. You said: "he can't paint."
I said: "well, I would dispute that but

49

at the least he grasps and envisions some of our reality
and your stuff is like... from another century..."

Most memorable: the visits to museums with you, for not only eastern but
western art. There an articulateness flowed forth.

There you were more perceptive than De Kooning and Bacon in
interviews. Your sardonic humor was tied in with seeing through man's
folly. The ghost of Goya appears in a glass enclosure as I think of how you,
a Socialist, might have updated his *Disasters of War* had you remained an
Expressionist...

*

Why, facing what many of us in some way faced,
being from Indianapolis, did a scythe-like undertow
ceaselessly move through you
as if charged by a remorse
your imagination was unable to deflect?

But we are all, at base, inscrutable, and similar,
maneuvered by rhinos
leading each of our skeletons about on a leash.

I speak of
the fumes of a man, of his soul grating,
what sticks:
     adherence to
a road with womb
that will never bear, but yields
late at night, with each motion of the baren,

driving the colors up into
    the vale of the hanga print makers:
huge knotted branch of
a Hokusai dragon,
cavernous with foaled void.

[September 2004–January 2006]

In the Seattle Art Museum, I stood before
"Good Morning, Mrs. Lincoln,"
Gorky testicles wiggling out of crab traps,
octopus pods dissolving into albino eels,
a vulva grail held forth by fingerless hands
to whom a penis-headed man, palm on hip,
displays his giant gully-raker (shades of
"The Artist and His Mother,"
of an emptied out Japanese Eros,
all *is* to be emptied out,
all is Easter razor, abstract libretto—
let the viewer restore the muscle tile,
"what am I doing in this menstrual hut in
the savannahs of Ivory Coast!"
he must cry out, "let me meet the holy fire
at the far edge of its scythe!").

Standing before Gorky that Lincoln afternoon,
I began to feel that wigwams lacked anaconda tiaras,
that in fetal gears there was no birch sugar,
that I was being served Aphrodite's pudenda
on an orchid by a blind man
on a lightless moor. I felt inspected by
pot-headed and deathless hybrids
or was it the four faces of Eve
making up the control panel of Cro-Magnon alarm?
Just then I felt the spider queen's beacon
sweep across man's gravid disasters of war!

Farewell, Mrs. Lincoln!—dear Gorky
just handed me a ticket for the Ivory Coast,
only a floor away, where the mask is the supreme court
and god festers forth from a swollen red
humanoid core.
                    Standing before this We mask,
I revisited Leon Golub's 1948 dilemma:
how grind Auschwitz simulacra
into a statement about power? Golub
transferred to the primitive, urging
what man had become to surface as the horror blender of
the extent to which the irrational dresses
mercs as presidents which too many accept
as the singing masters of their souls.
This nameless mask from We
milked and repumped my Orestial maidens,
I found in one long feeler a Bashō straw, and,
sucking in a compote of cicada-absorbed rock
re-entered the earth of the *Shah-nameh*
where all is alive, pink ground quilted with
tufts of violet grass, clouds like entangled
cork-screwing silver snakes, miniver rose formations
alive as coral reefs. The horrendous is just
one polecat in the anagrams of the molework
we attempt to unscramble in dreams.
Yet the force in the face of god
as a beltway of circulating thrashers
in the bandsaw of a shark's eye
stayed with me. It said:
imaginal density is greater than you have conceived.
What most take poetry to be

is at best an ortolan hors d'oeuvre.
On the far side of the muse
there are cometary knots
in which a Tarantula Nebula is volatilizing
with all its tarantella power
spit like fire through facial
groin-horned snake-pouched feelers.

Then Caryl and I left,
drank a Washington State Chinook Cabernet
and thanked Dionysus for a glacial day.

[for John and Roberta Olson]

How pay homage to the marvelous Unica Zürn?

Her mental centipedes, the gurry of death, the web
coming alive as it frays. Impossible,
no matter, impossible, and in no matter
the impossible is alive. Lines as notes
in a musical structure, eyes snarled
in totemic compression, like glyphs,
or Jurassic sea lilies moored to the sea floor.
Behold the revenge of "There is no place that does not see you"—
did Rilke realize what anxiety he was tapping?

The air, the air has fangs, it tiptoes on its tail toe,
flexing its exit window,
a sac being filled with micro-organic charm,
the polyp-filled air! the goiter-backed air!
amoebic with the soup of pre-worlds,
curling, snapping ferny worms!

In the *Shah-nameh*, grotesque animals and human faces show through
rocks and verdure. Are these presences the buried but still alive energy
deposits of a deep past, kin to Greek Titans encased in Tartarus? Unica
Zürn appears to have intuited a variation not only on the 16th century
Persian masterpiece but on the wily tradition of the grotesque, displaying
a mind embedded with the eyeful dead, cross-phylum-dressers, the
elemental automata Kenneth Grant writes, that "if fed by lunar vibrations
or substantiated by means of sexual magick will breed an actual entity
from the depths."

In the art of Unica Zürn, the known is redearranged,
the red-eared angel is crushed into a thousand eyes,
as if in Tantrik diffraction, cranial shapes
break into heads in telescopic profiles, with eye lozenge
clusters of hanging pods. Abyss weevils
percolate with seed energies.
Drawing as multiplying cells, chert complexes
milling with atavistic surge.
To travel within Unica's tear, to view the celestial
viper-vibrational
xylophone of her mind, the cartwheel
cocoliths of her insectile-thronging dark.
Eyes as trowels.
Raccoon nautiloids in millipedal waver.
Her art burgeons off its own zoa, beholden only to
the stamina of its rhizomes.
Line mines with off-shoot eye shafts,
gorges flexing on an orgy's
whimpering forge.

"Who," Unica asks, "will choose me?
I am inside Atlas, stranded in birth channel,
without birth-father peristaltic push.
For friends I have Owl-Eyed Midge, Bird in Eye-Bra,
Night Sea of Scowling White Eyes,
Mr. Cat with Rivets instead of Hair.
As I draw I fall, the charge is to swerve right before
pupilizing the void. I ascend, whir like a wraith on a lathe,
sometimes a drawing is no more than my exhaust.
Always the implied concussion,
never closure with flags.

In the outback of the face,
which shadow womb will burst into
faceted eye-mazed extra-terrestriality?
Is it yours, Michaux? Or has Bellmer again divided into
Herman Bells and Ellen Brahms?
As long as I am crawled by moss animals,
I can masturbate and knot my nipples with aquatic centipedes.
Never has become a location. Hans and Unica
anagrammed as: Carnalizes Humbler Nun.
Brazen Lumenal Urchins. These are my marriage vows, my
graphic juxtapositioned fissions, my
Xibalba eyeball ping pong.

Today I face a fish face made of two faces facing away,
male half-heads in profile joined.
At the seam a nostril appears, and a mouth
slithering with smile. Standing on this trophy:
a disintegrating muse. Occasionally she appears,
an organ of sorts, floating out from my body,
attached by a stringy gland...
an astronaut on the umbilicus of the Tarantula Nebula...
I'm losing my contours, I'm stepping out to where
nullity comeuppance knocks itself up."

"A bootful of brain
set out in the rain"

—that is Paul Celan, Paris, 1969.
Could have been a GI snapshot, Vietnam.

Leon Golub rounded up four boots,
grew military torturer legs in them,
shiny brown pedestals on which
outside my bedroom door
a naked man hanging upside down is being whacked.

The avant-garde: the first upon the scene,
while the crime is still blazing, in Laverdant's 1848 definition:
"those who lay bare, with a brutal brush,
all the brutalities, all the filth, which are at the base of society."
The core of Golub's career is in its complex response to annihilation.
His comrades-in-arm are Goya at the Judas peephole
refusing to avert his gaze; Callot with his lynch tree, become
Billie Holiday's "strange fruit;" Dix's *Trench*; Picasso's *Guernica*;
Heartfield's angels in gas masks intoning:
"O du fröhliche, o du selige, gnadenbringende Zeit!"

1946: to transform the water-filled, wreckage-laden basement of
Western culture into a primordial bath,
a deep rolling masked blackness in milling assembly,
fangs studding the abstract with wilderness eyes.
Burnt, bird-legged Hamlet paws the air.

Golub sphinxes: half-swallowed, half-born, from *sphincter*,
orifice of the contracting angel, the nightmare choker.
How much degradation can an image take
and still, scraped into and from the canvas itself, manifest
this world's lethal embrace? The age
demanded an image, right? ok? here it is:
man as ruined monumentality. Reclining Youth:
his surface spatter mimicked by wound-trailed ground,
the limb-ghosted ground mimicked by white bone-like finality.
Gigantomachies: gods fighting in accelerated grimace,
syncopation of drunken, flayed cargo sloshing in an indestructable hold.

The Golub archetypal question:
if abstract color fields are peeled away,
what terrors will show through?

Golub's torturers know we accept their actions
as they accept our passive regard.
For most of us watch them from behind the great religious systems of
    compensatory evasion.

Golub asks: "Is it possible to export destruction, to burn and drive peasants
from their homes, and maintain the dream of the perfectibility of art?
Well, it is possible if art concerns itself with itself and does not dare to
presume political meaning." (1969)

This is mental war, intellectual, determined
that art be somehow commensurate with international event.
Golub's South African blacks,
the chorus of a lifework, watch him and occasionally break into threnody.
They watch you, viewer, as do the Salvadoran white squads

stuffing car trunks with the corpse you will never escape.
The power principle behind evil,
so deeply a matter of the unconscious now
as to not know its own name, "down there,"
in close combat blood galaxies,
where one plus one is always one, a zero rack
encrusted with victimized rage.

A Golubian vision of the American flag:
napalm-blistered stripes so star-mangled they resonate burnt blue.

Oh fatality of expectation and freedom!
(Where other Americans saw angels beaming at Reagan,
Golub saw Contras destroying Nicaraguan grain silos, health centers,
    cutting off women's breasts)

In old age,
touched by death, the hand of the master sets free the fractured
    landscape,
the goal dims, a shredder abyss moves in,
dissociation tears apart time.
Skeletons wear the pants in the house of being.
Night street nodes of slicks, glare and wash out
mesh in crystalline smear.
Has any other artist ever depicted the zone of closure more trenchantly?
Golub in the underworld at 80,
still facing America's will to administer absolutely,
but now the prey of dogs, eagles, and lions,
as if man the predator had once again become prey.
Slogans honk, lit tableaux in a tunnel of horror.
"Another joker out of business" "Raptor sanction"

Foresight becomes gore right. A sparagmos of the torn and the tearer.
Pink dog tongue fused dick diddling a female spectre.
In the new armpit showcase, skeletons toast hounds.
"Transmission garbled."
                    Leon Golub exits.
              Now in my mind indelible,
    the corrosive flicker from his unstanchable wound.

                              [March-April, 2005]

FURTHER NOTES
&
APPENDIX

"Figure and Ground": The idea for this poem occurred while reading Declan McGonagle's Foreword to Jon Bird's *Leon Golub / Echoes of the Real* (Reaktion Books, London, 2000). McGonagle writes: "The contest in art is regularly characterized, and trivialized, by the media as a contest between forms of figuration and abstraction when the fundamental tension is actually between figure and ground—the figure of art/the artist and the ground of society... the figure is never actually lost in Golub's paintings, as it is in Byzantine or Islamic art, where the ground/the collective becomes more important than the figure/the individual. I would argue that Golub, as a citizen-artist, argues the need for both the individual and the collective aspects of humanity to be upheld in a tension that is fundamentally democratic because it is inclusive and acknowledges its origins in culture as well as nature."

"Michaux, 1956": Giorgio Agamben focused my attention on the word "whatever" in the opening essay in *The Coming Community* (The University of Minnesota Press, 2000). In the poem "Q," in *The Promises of Glass* (New Directions, 2000), Michael Palmer, possibly inspired by Agamben's fascination with the word, plays off the Latin *quodlibet* ("whatever"), and creates a character named "Quod."

"Chauvet: Left Wall of End Chamber": With James O'Hern, I visited the Chauvet Cave with Jean-Marie Chauvet (one of the three 1994 discoverers) on January 8, 2004. My gratitude to Dominique Baffier for arranging our visit. Excellent color photographs of the wall with the paintings addressed in my poem may be found in *Chauvet Cave / The Art of Earliest Times*, directed by Jean Clottes (The University of Utah Press, Salt Lake City, 2003).

"Some of Her Names": This poem is a revision of a poem in an unpublished manuscript, "Our Journey Around the Drowned City of Is," which was based on trips to French Brittany in 1985 and 1987. Via Nantes, we entered the Brittany peninsula, and over the next three weeks (in 1985), drove around it, paying special attention to the megaliths in the Carnac area, the fissured cliffs of Finistère, the ominous Arrée Mountains, and the beautiful pink granite of the Bretonne Corniche. I was half-way through the writing of *Juniper Fuse: Upper Paleolithic Imagination & the Construction of the Underworld* while on this trip, and a second one, two years later, and I saw the stones, dolmens, and menhirs in Brittany as a groundwork for building imaginative links between the ancient decorated caves and modern history.

"The Beheading": I am indebted to Peter Robb's rethinking of Caravaggio's life and art in *M / The Man Who Became Caravaggio* (Picador USA, 2001—my quote is from that book, p. 437), as well as to Catherine Puglisi's excellent *Caravaggio* (Phaidon, London, 2000), with its detailed investigation of "The Beheading of Saint John the Baptist," and to Leo Bersani and Ulysse Dutoit's *Caravaggio's Secrets* (an OCTOBER Book, Cambridge, 1998), with its sensitive scrutiny of many paintings. I am also in debt to Dominic Cutajar, not only for his essay, "Caravaggio in Malta" (from *Malta and Caravaggio*, Malta, 1986), but also for asking the Oratory guards in Valletta's Co-Cathedral to turn off the two alarm systems so that Caryl and I, along with our friends James Heller Levinson and Victoria Ganim, could almost touch the twelve by seventeen foot "Beheading" with our noses, in May 2002.

"Radix": Khaled Al-Saa'i is a young Syrian painter/calligrapher currently living and showing in Dubai. Caryl and I discovered his art in a show at the University of Michigan Art Museum in 2002. He is a kind of Arabic calligraphic "action painter," who creates "fields" of improvisational Arabic calligraphic mindscapes. From what we can tell, his work is extraordinary and unique, and like nothing in contemporary American painting.

"Unica Zürn": The German artist Unica Zürn (1916-1970) appears to have begun to draw after becoming the companion of Hans Bellmer (1902-1975), in Paris in 1953, undoubtedly stimulated by Bellmer's darkly erotic and meticulous art. While in Paris she had contact with some of the Surrealists, like Breton and Matta, and is said to have been introduced to mescaline by Henri Michaux (who she referred to as "The Jasmine Man" in one of her several books). In *Sulfur #29* (1991), Renée Riese Hubert edited a 40 page section of Zürn's texts and drawings. She committed suicide in 1970, via defenestration, at the couple's Paris apartment.

In the spring of 2004, we visited a show of some 70 of her drawings at the Ubu Gallery in NYC. Up to that point, I had a rather hazy image of her as a drawer, and mainly thought of her as Bellmer's disturbed companion. But this show revealed that her art belongs with the best that Surrealism has to offer. She is, in my opinion, the peer of Matta, Michaux, Ernst, Varo, Hoch, and Kahlo. I brought home a catalog from the Ubu Gallery show, *Unica Zürn / Bilder 1953-1970* (Verlag Brinkman und Bose / Neue Gesellschaft für Bildende Kunst / Berlin 1998), with reproductions of over 200 drawings, and over the next two months wrote two pieces off Zürn's "combined objects." This is the shorter, and more introductory, of the two.

"Monumental": Through March and April, in 2005, I worked on a piece for the public memorial program for the painter Leon Golub, who had died at 82 in August, 2004, at Cooper Union's Great Hall, in NYC. Golub is one of the greatest of American painters, and his painterly trackings of our horrendous overseas government involvements in torture and murder throughout the 60's, 70's, 80's, and 90's, are acts of courageous witnessing. The last twenty-five years of Golub's paintings are the closest thing we have in America to Goya's "black period" and *The Disasters of War*. No wonder no major museum in the New York City area has ever given him a retrospective: his moral acuity cuts like acid through the evasion and lies that have become our public and aesthetic policy.

My earliest recollections of involvement with the visual arts goes back to reading the "funnies" in daily Indianapolis newspapers, collecting comic books, and drawing my own cartoon strips. When I was around 10 years old, my mother offered an art student from the Herron School of Art a free dinner and a couple of dollars to give me and my pal Jack Wilson weekly cartoon lessons. I vaguely recall one of my cartoons winning a prize at some contest in a department store. In my junior and senior years at Shortridge High School, I took some figure drawing classes and did quite well in them. I did a drawing of a hobo who had been paid to pose that my mother put up on our living room wall for many years. I think I might have become a painter had there been a more intense art atmosphere to involve myself with in Indianapolis at the time.

My mother also arranged for me to take piano lessons from a neighborhood piano teacher when I was 6 years old, and the lessons continued up through my teenage years when, on one hand, I was playing Chopin's "Revolutionary Etude," and, on the other, starting to hang out at local blues and jazz clubs, such as The Surf Club on West 16th Street where one Saturday afternoon I was invited to "sit in" with Wes Montgomery and his brothers. In the summer of 1953, when I was working as a life guard at The Riviera Club, I met John Fish, who had recently gotten out of the army and had bought a black 1953 Lincoln convertible. Fish loved jazz and proposed that we take off and go to Los Angeles where there was a flourishing West Coast "scene." I ended up parking cars at a Systems Auto Park in downtown LA, and studying piano with Marty Paitch and Richie Powell. One night Fish and I spotted a couple of gorgeous African-American women after parking our car in the Tiffany Club parking lot, and tried to pick them up. It turned out they were the wives (or girlfriends) of Clifford Brown and Max Roach who were playing there that week.

I mention some of this musical history here as part of the background that resulted in my starting to write poetry at Indiana University in 1957. I put myself through graduate school by playing at a piano bar in the Dandale restaurant on the downtown Bloomington Square, and while doing so, I realized my talent in music was limited. I think one reason that it was limited was because it was too tied up with being from Indianapolis and being part of a life that one way or the other I had to overturn. Poetry was something I discovered on my own, and it held a vista that almost immediately opened onto the discovery of the poetry of Pablo Neruda and César Vallejo, and subsequent hitch-hiking trips to Mexico.

I think that the first poems I wrote about art works attempted to engage Picasso's "Guernica" and Bosch's "Garden of Earthly Delights." I wrote these as a student in Sam Yellen's creative writing course at Indiana University and I no longer have a copy of either poem.

Previous to this collection of poems, I have, over the years, published a number of poems about paintings, drawings, sculpture and artists in my various books. What follows is a list of what I have been able to track down:

from WALKS (1967):
Walk VII (the Rafael Larco Herrera Museum in Lima, Peru)

from INDIANA (1969):
The Matisse 1914 *Colligure*
Soutine (the art of Chaim Soutine)

from COILS (1973):
Coils (material on Coatlicue)

from THE GULL WALL (1975):
  Gargoyles
  Creation (the Venus of Lespugue)
  Portrait of Vincent Van Gogh
  Portrait of Chaim Soutine
  "Leon Golub working on a painting"
  Portrait of Francis Bacon

from WHAT SHE MEANS (1978):
  Study for a Portrait of Hans Bellmer
  Les Combarelles
  Dialogue with a Triptych (by Francis Bacon)

from HADES IN MANGANESE (1981):
  Cato's Altars (the art of Bob Cato)
  Frida Kahlo's Release
  Dot (Upper Paleolithic imagery)
  Hades in Manganese (descent into the Upper Paleolithic)
  Meditation on Marwan's Faces (the art of Marwan Kassabachi)
  Etruscan Vase
  From St.-Cirq to Caravaggio
  Tartaros (engravings at Les Trois Frères)
  Our Lady of the Three-Pronged Devil (ancient vulva engravings)

from FRACTURE (1983):
  A Small Cave (Bernifal)
  Magdalenian ("The Shameless Venus")
  All of the poems in "II / The Paleolithic Dimension"
  All of the poems in "III / Tomb of Donald Duck"
  Elegy (material on Caravaggio)

from THE NAME ENCANYONED RIVER (1986):
Nora Jaffe
Tuxedoed Groom on Canvas Bride (the art of Max Beckmann)

from HOTEL CRO-MAGNON (1989):
Kerlescan, 1985 (the Carnac standing stones)
Kerlescan, 1987
Menhirs
At the Cleveland Museum of Art
Still-Life with Grapes & Pears
On Atget's Road (the photography of Eugène Atget)
Pan's Signal Tower (after a painting by David True)
Ode to the Man in the Moon (after a painting by Frida Kahlo)
Galactite (In Memory of Ana Mendieta)

from UNDER WORLD ARREST (1994)
The Power Room (Les Eyzies Regional Prehistory Museum)
Venusberg
Some Fugal Lubrication (Drachenloch)
Humbaba
Like Violets, He Said (Lascaux)
Guyton Place (the art of Tyree Guyton)

from FROM SCRATCH (1998):
Prolegomena (Neanderthal cupules at La Ferrassie)
de Kooning's *Woman I*
Self-Portrait by a Cameroon Mask
Nora's Roar (the art of Nora Jaffe)
Shmatte Variations (based on the dolls of Michel Nedjar)
Register's Beyond (the art of John Register)
de Kooning's *February*

72

Oy (the art of Chaim Soutine)

Soutine's Lapis

On a Photograph of Gall

I, Friedrich Schröder-Sonnenstern

A Phosphene Gauntlet

Le Combel

Indeterminate, Open (parietal human figurations of the Combarelles
cave)

de Kooning's *Excavation (I)*

de Kooning's *Excavation (II)*

Matrix, Blower (the Venuses of Laussel and Lespugue)

JUNIPER FUSE: UPPER PALEOLITHIC IMAGINATION &
THE CONSTRUCTION OF THE UNDERWORLD (2003):
Much of the material in this study appeared in earlier collections,
often in earlier versions, and has been noted above.

from MY DEVOTION (2004):
Sparks We Trail (a painting in Lascaux)
The Hybrid is the Engine of Anima Display (engravings at Les Trois
Frères)
Erratics (sections on Hans Bellmer, Dalí, Sheela-na-Gig, ancient hand
negatives, Lascaux's "Chinese Horse," Nancy Spero, Jackson
Pollock, and Peter Beard).

Clayton Eshleman (Indianapolis, 1935)
has distinguished himself as a poet, essayist,
translator, editor, and paleo-archeologist.
From 1968 to 2004, Black Sparrow Press
published 14 collections of his poetry. He
has published two collections of essays,
and a third will appear in 2007. He is the
main American translator of César Vallejo,
Antonin Artaud, and Aimé Césaire (he
has also translated Michel Deguy, Pablo

Neruda, and Vladimir Holan). He founded and edited two of the most
seminal literary journals of the 20th century: *Caterpillar* (1967-1973, 20
issues) and *Sulfur* (1981-2000, 46 issues). From 1974 to 1999, he researched
the Ice Age painted caves of southwestern France, the fruits of which is
Juniper Fuse: Upper Paleolithic Imagination & the Construction of the Underworld
(Wesleyan University Press, 2003). He has received a number of awards,
including a National Book Award, the Landon Translation Prize, a
Guggenheim Fellowship, a Rockefeller Study Center Residency, and
four grants from the National Endowment for the Arts and the National
Endowment for the Humanities. Since 1996, he and his wife Caryl have
led a journey yearly to the Ice Age painted caves in the French Dordogne,
sponsored by the Ringling School of Art in Sarasota. He continues to live
in Ypsilanti, Michigan, where he is a Professor Emeritus in the English
Department of Eastern Michigan University.

DESIGN BY MICHAEL KOSHKIN & JENNIFER ROGERS
TYPESET IN GOUDY OLD STYLE
PRINTED BY MCNAUGHTON & GUNN
ON RECYCLED (50% POST CONSUMER WASTE), ACID-FREE PAPER

hOt whiskey pess